AF412379

This is the story of . . . Little John
Fly Me to the Moon!

story by Valerie Gale ● characters illustrated by David Hohn ● edited by PJ Putnam

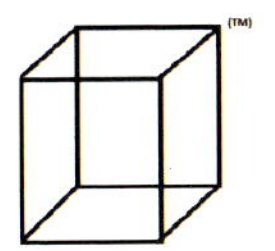

Edutainment Press

Written by Valerie Gale
Characters originally designed and illustrated by David Hohn
Illustrations by Liquid Development, LLC

Edited by PJ Putnam

Published by Edutainment Press, an imprint of Mantup Enterprises, LLC

Printed in the United States of America

We selected our printing facilities with care. This book was printed in the USA using soy-based ink. The paper includes 10% post-consumer waste (PCW) recycled content; and, is Forest Stewardship Council (FSC), Sustainable Forest Initiative (SFI) and Programme for the Endorsement of Forest certification (PEFC) certified. The book meets or exceeds all CPSIA guidelines for Pthalate Lead Content.

The two photographs used in the history section are from the NASA Archives. For further information or assistance regarding NASA, you may contact:

NASA Headquarters
Office of Public Affairs
Media Services Division
News and Imaging Branch
Code PM
300 E St., SW
Washington, DC 29546
Telephone: (202) 358-1900

Edutainment Press, 5909 London Court, Dallas, TX 75252
(214) 449-0566 - www.edutainmentpress.com

Library of Congress Cataloging-in-Publication data is on-file with the publisher

ISBN: 978-0-9839093-0-9

Dedicated in honor and memory of my grandparents -- Gramma, Dido and Baba — for their commitment to dreams and persistence. For leaving a legacy of excellence.
-Valerie Gale, Author

To my wonderful children — may you always look at the moon and know that it is within your reach.

-PJ Putnam, Editor and Publisher

Preface

It's been said that "a word fitly spoken is like apples of silver in settings of gold" . . . And I believe it! I always have. For as long as I can remember, I have surrounded myself either deliberately or instinctively with positive words. As a child, I recall the picture in my room graced with two simple words . . . "press on". . . and then the poster on my door declaring that as a little girl born on a Sunday - I was destined to be "fair, and wise . . . and good" . . . and "happy."

As years passed . . . I found that words came naturally to me - whether written or spoken - I could often be found writing cards or stories, notes of love or gratitude, prose and poetry. And, then those same words even more easily converted to speech, to the point where before I knew it, gifts of silver and gold seemed to have crept their way into my very being - oozing through my fingertips and lingering on my lips.

And, what I've come to learn . . . is that *words carry great power*. They have the ability to build up or deflate, to bring life or to torture the minds and hearts of those we love or despise. When uttered in kindness - words motivate and invigorate - and when spoken silently though writing - they may be treasured, wrapped up . . . and put away to be saved for another day - when they are needed once again to lift, soothe, comfort and inspire.

It is the power of positive words . . . in my own life - that led me to believe early on that nothing was impossible . . . that dreams are made for realizing and that life is a game to be played inning after inning . . . round after round, quarter after quarter . . . turn after turn - whether painful or pleasant.

Unfortunately, I also recognize that many children do not experience this same infusion of energy (that is, the gift of words and motivation). Many adults I know have never realized the power of words to produce the drive and enthusiasm for goals and life. But when I meet someone who has these gifts, I am instantly drawn to that person. And, I want to learn, listen to that person and be further motivated and inspired. And that is how this story - of a boy - was born.

Lessons in Life and Leadership for Kids is about providing children with stories that are steeped in history and rich with encouragement, comfort, inspiration, challenge and motivation. I believe that now is the time; our homes and schools are the place where we must take hold of our opportunities to infuse these priceless gifts of life in our children — who are the future leaders of our world. To build others through developing and growing and coaching them to greatness . . . is the purpose.

So whether you are reading this book as a parent, teacher, babysitter, big brother or sister, aunt or uncle - my hope is that this story not only infuses energy into the life of the child you are reading to, but that it also ignites a fire within you. Life is life . . . so make today the day you set fire to the rain . . . take hold of the light within and press forward to pursue what only you can.

The world is waiting . . . don't make it wait another moment.

Valerie Gale, Author, July 20, 2011

Foreword

I must express my sincere gratitude to Valerie Gale for writing this gripping and inspiring story about two young people, determined to realize their dreams, committed success and to each other. Her ability to capture the heart and imagination of readers through her words is remarkable. I anticipate that readers of all ages will be naturally drawn to the story of Little John and Little Jo in a way that will cause them to examine their own lives, goals, dreams and accomplishments.

This book evokes many fine awakenings for children and grown-ups alike. In this story, we become acquainted and fall in love with Little John and Little Jo. The first implication of this, is that young people become aware of life and the importance of realizing their goals. Secondly, it would be my hope that parents and educators alike would make use of this book as a learning tool in the classroom and at home, encouraging children to emulate the positive characteristics of both Little John and Little Jo.

As an educator and counselor, I believe this book sheds a creative light on the discovery of history, while also demonstrating and encouraging appreciation for what one can become. The lessons woven throughout the story become a baton to be passed along to the next "learner" as a guide for the steps to take in life.

Here are some of the valuable areas of discovery contained in this story:

- how can I satisfy my need to feel significant?

- how can I conquer my fears and emotions and persevere to accomplish my goals?

- if I have a broken ambition or dream, can I have another chance?

- how can my life truly make a difference?

I am excited to see how this book will transform the perspective of young people and inspire them to do the impossible.

Dr. Myrtle Hightower
Retired Counselor - Plano Independent School District
President - Plano Community Charity

Little John was always dreaming . . .

He was always planning . . .

Always thinking and . . .

always learning.

Little John was always looking for ways to make the world a better place.

He was always fair, always kind, and most of the time . . . he was wise.

As most little boys do, Little John liked to be the hero!

He liked to be a hero at school. He liked to be a hero at recess. And, he liked to be a hero at home.

But most of all when he was sleeping . . . he was a hero in his dreams.

He was a hero on land . . . he was a hero at sea . . . and, he was a hero in space . . . .

On land, he fought and won wars - defeating the dragons and expanding his kingdom.

At sea, he traveled far below the surface of the ocean and discovered treasures aplenty.

But of all the dreams he had . . . his dream of being a hero in space seemed the hardest to reach.

Perhaps that was because nobody had ever been to space . . .

it was deep and it was dark and it was *ohhhh so high!*

But, late at night as Little John looked out his window to stare at the moon and the stars . . .

he dreamed this biggest dream of all!

As you can imagine, Little John was so busy being a hero and a dreamer
that he didn't have much time for anything or anyone else.

While most of the other children were playing tag or hide & seek,
Little John was planning his trip to the moon.

Little John's friends thought nothing of his dreaming. "Just come and play" they would say. And, "forget your silly dreams."

But Little John **never quit**!

One night as Little John began to slip into a deep sleep, a curious and beautiful girl arrived in his dream.

She was so pretty and resembled Little Jo from his kindergarten class.

Because Little John was so happy to have some company, he let her stay there . . . in his dream.
After all, he could always use some help getting his spacesuit zipped up . . .
and, the latch on his helmet *was* a little tricky.

And so, there they were, Little John and Little Jo getting ready to head to the moon.

Little Jo carefully made sandwiches for Little John's moon picnic.
She folded his map, and she folded his extra spacesuit.

She made sure Little John had everything he needed for the long trip into space.

But before Little John climbed up into his spaceship,
Little Jo gave him a hug, a kiss on the nose and a final thumbs up.

When at last, it was time to go . . . Little Jo watched him latch the door and she waved good-bye . . .

As Little John quickly disappeared from sight, Little Jo whispered a prayer
that he would make it safely to the moon and back.

Before long, Little John was high, high, high up in space.
There were more stars than he ever imagined . . .

and the moon – *oh, the moon, it was so beautiful!!*

When Little John reached the moon, he parked his spaceship and climbed out of the capsule

to take pictures . . . and, to have his picnic.

But as beautiful as the moon was, it wasn't long before Little John began wishing Little Jo was with him.
After all, she had folded his map and packed his extra spacesuit . . .
she had even made his favorite sandwiches for the picnic.

Little Jo was the one person who had believed that he would make it all the way to the moon!

While eating his lonely moon picnic, Little John *knew* that he had to head back home.
The moon was a lovely picnic spot; but, home was where his heart was . . .

and, where he would find Little Jo.

Before Little John repacked his rocket for the voyage home,
he carved a message onto the crust of the moon . . . .

Then, Little John jumped back into his spaceship, revved its engines, and headed back home.

He zoomed past the stars and past the sun, through dark skies and blue skies . . .

until finally, he could see the ground below.

Then as the clouds cleared, Little John saw Little Jo standing just where he left her.
She was still looking up into the sky . . .

And, where she was earlier waving goodbye, she is now waving hello!

And as the spaceship landed and its door opened, Little John raced down the mile-long stairs
to find Little Jo jumping up and down in excitement.

"Tell me, tell me all about it!" she exclaimed.

And, so, he did.

And they sat and they sat for hours. Talking and dreaming, dreaming and talking!

As nighttime fell in Little John's dream, he realized it would soon be time to say good-bye once again to Little Jo. But before he said goodnight to her, Little John stopped long enough to look her straight in the eyes and he asked her two important questions . . .

And, as his eyelids fluttered open from sleep to day, he heard Little Jo say,
"I helped and I waited 'cause *I believed in you;* and, I just *knew* you'd make it to the moon and back."

With those words, Little John got up from his bed and got ready for school
with more energy and more excitement than ever before.

He was a hero in his dreams and in this world . . .
on land . . .
at sea . . .
and finally . . .
in space!

Parents and Educators – Background Information on
President John F. Kennedy and his goal to put a Man on the Moon!

"I look forward to a great future for America – a future in which our country will match its military strength with our moral restraint, its wealth with our wisdom, its power with our purpose" - JFK

On July 20, 1969, astronauts Neil Armstrong and Buzz Aldrin became the first humans to land on the moon during the Apollo 11 spaceflight mission. The Apollo 11 mission was conducted by National Aeronautics and Space Administration (NASA) and launched from Florida on July 16, 1969. The American Astronauts spent over twenty one hours on the surface of the moon and returned to earth with forty seven pounds of lunar rock. Apollo 11 returned to earth and landed in the Pacific Ocean on July 24, 1969. The Apollo 11 mission symbolized a major global accomplishment for NASA, space exploration and the United States. Furthermore, the mission's success fulfilled President John F. Kennedy's goal that America would land a human on the moon before the Soviet Union. NASA successfully landed five additional Apollo spaceflights on the moon between 1969 and 1972. America had once again achieved greatness through exploration, overcoming tremendous challenges and pursuing our dreams of making the world a better place.

(Photo from the NASA Archives. At 9:32 a.m. EDT, the swing arms move away and a plume of flame signals the liftoff of the Apollo 11 Saturn V space vehicle and astronauts Neil A. Armstrong, Michael Collins and Edwin E. Aldrin, Jr. from Kennedy Space Center Launch Complex 39A.)

President John Fitzgerald Kennedy set these actions in motion. On May 25, 1961, President Kennedy addressed Congress with his ambitious plan to be the first country to put a man on the moon. Members of Congress and other leaders around the world doubted that the idea was even possible. Kennedy pressed on. In his famous address to the United States Congress in 1961, he expressed, *"I believe that this nation should commit itself to achieving the goal, before this decade is out, of landing a man on the moon and returning him safely to earth."*

(Photo from the NASA Archives. Dr. Wernher von Braun explains the Saturn Launch System to President John F. Kennedy. NASA Deputy Administrator Robert Seamans is to the left of von Braun.)

President Kennedy believed that putting a man on the moon symbolized America's unwavering dedication to greatness. This daunting task also represented our commitment as a nation to achieve knowledge through exploration. Above all, the visionary President believed that Americans could inspire the entire world by accomplishing this never done before mission. He believed that we could inspire nations and its people to believe in their dreams and never concede that something is impossible.

First Lady, Jacqueline Kennedy recognized the President's passion to accomplish this mission by signing letters to the President that would read, *"I love you to the moon and back – your dearest Jacqueline"*.

President Kennedy knew that putting a man on the moon would not win the war on poverty or cool relations with the Soviet Union, but he understood that the world needed America to land on the moon because the world desperately needed a great America.

In a speech at Rice University, President Kennedy proclaimed:

"We choose to go to the Moon in this decade and do the other things, not because they are easy, but because they are hard, because that goal will serve to organize and measure the best of our energies and skills, because that challenge is one that we are willing to accept, one we are unwilling to postpone, and one which we intend to win, and the others, too . . .

Many years ago the great British explorer George Mallory, who was to die on Mount Everest, was asked why did he want to climb it. He said, "Because it is there." Well, space is there, and we're going to climb it, and the Moon and the planets are there, and new hopes for knowledge and peace are there. And, therefore, as we set sail we ask God's blessing on the most hazardous and dangerous and greatest adventure on which man has ever embarked."

Every child grows up with dreams and aspirations to be great. Some may dream of becoming an astronaut, others, a fireman or policeman, a school teacher, a professional athlete or perhaps, even the President of the United States. As adults, we should not merely encourage these ideas; we must illuminate the possibilities. One of the most beautiful things about young children is their unmatched ability to reach for the impossible. Just like President John F. Kennedy dreamed to put a man on the moon – the impossible became very possible.

So, whether you are a young boy growing up in a big city like Dallas, New York, Los Angeles or Chicago or you're a young girl growing up in the small American towns of Boone, Iowa, Flint, Michigan or Tazewell, Virginia, the entire country and people all over the world are depending on you to dream big and live your life working to fulfill your dreams. These dreams are the future of our world, so dream to the moon and back because that is where you will find greatness . . .

-- Contributing Writer – Mark Greer

NOTE to Parents and Educators: please take an opportunity to highlight for your children (or students) the **lessons in life and leadership for kids ("L3FK")** in this story:

- **L3FK #1: Importance of setting goals/having dreams**
  At any age and in any stage of life, setting goals and allowing yourself to "dream big" is very important. But, it is difficult to get somewhere you have never visited before without a map. Often times, goals and dreams will serve as *your* map. As it is with life; if you don't take the time to set goals and dream dreams, it will be harder for you realize them come true.

- **L3FK #2: Be yourself – have courage to persevere**
  Mark Twain once said, "stay away from people who try to belittle [or, make fun of] your ambitions. Small people always do that, but the really great make you feel that you, too, can become great." Friends may try to discourage you when you are playing a sport, learning to play an instrument or just trying to finish your homework. Whatever your task is – be yourself and be courageous to finish what you start. If you make a promise – like President Kennedy did – do everything within your power to keep your promise.

- **L3FK #3: Choose your friends wisely, for two is better than one**
  Just as Little John had Little Jo by his side, helping and encouraging him along on his journey, you too need good friends that will stick by you. In our story, Little Jo was good at the things that Little John wasn't good at doing. She planned the trip and prepared him for his long journey. *He just wanted to travel to space.* Can you imagine if he had arrived on the moon for his picnic without a picnic lunch? Don't forget how important it is to choose good friends that help make you better; life is sweeter when it is shared.

Acknowledgements

As this dream of mine has come to fruition, my heart and mind is overwhelmed with gratitude. For along the journey that has been my life - I can look back now and recognize how God carefully orchestrated each moment and each interaction with so many people who would play a critical role in not only developing and shaping who I am - but also encouraging my achievements and aspirations. And so, at the risk of leaving someone out....please bear with me as I attempt to articulate my gratitude...

To my parents - *Dan and Gale* - at times words come easily....yet now they seem inadequate to convey all that you mean to me. Your constant and unwavering love has been a consistent source of strength and "fuel" in my life that kept a fire burning deep within me to be and do all that was possible.... I will never be able to thank you enough. To my remarkable children - *Abi and Mac*, thank you for being the first two people to hear the story....and see it in your minds... and fall in love with Little John and Little Jo. You are the gifts most undeserved in my life....and I simply couldn't be the person that I am without you both. To *Caroline, Angie, Amye, Krista, Kari and Kim* for reading and re-reading and for looking at character sketches on iPads and iPhones, smiling and listening, dreaming with and being proud of me - your friendship and support has been an absolute treasure....

To *Rob* for taking time that you didn't have...for your tireless review of each and every picture, and critical detail - for recognizing the potential for the book to have a real impact in the lives of kids - and for your business mind to work leading the rest of the team.... To my Illustrators at **Liquid Development, LLC** in Portland, OR, thank you from the top of my head to the tips of my toes for your creative genius.... for reading my mind in developing the character's personalities and for magically making the words on the page come alive. And to *PJ Putnam* - my "Leadership Plano bus partner" - turned friend - turned publisher ... thank you for believing that this story had real possibility - for walking me through this every step of the way ... and patiently watching as this all came to be - I am so grateful to you.

To my entire family, including *Christopher and Audrey, Catherine, Jennifer and Quinn,* as well as many nieces and nephews, trusted friends and mentors, please accept my appreciation for your influence and infilling in my life... So many of you have used your words and hearts to communicate your faith and confidence in me as a person, a professional, a friend, a mom.... And I recognize from the deepest part of me - that dreams are not realized alone - and that the death of one dream....can fuel hope in another.

I am beyond thankful for each of you and to the God who made me for life and living.... *Valerie Gale*